TO THE
BONEYARD

BARBARA MARSH

TO THE BONE – YARD

EYEWEAR PUBLISHING

First published in 2013
by Eyewear Publishing Ltd
74 Leith Mansions, Grantully Road
London w9 1lj
United Kingdom

Typeset with graphic design by Edwin Smet
Author photograph by S. Parkhill and A. Kjaergaard
Printed in England by TJ International Ltd, Padstow, Cornwall

ISBN 978-1-908998-12-5

WWW.EYEWEARPUBLISHING.COM

For Steve

and dedicated to the memory of Ruth Stone

Barbara Marsh lives and teaches in London.
Born in Rhode Island, USA, she spent her childhood traversing
America with her family due to her father's Naval career. After
university, she lived in New York City as a singer/songwriter (and
bartender), making inroads into the Village music scene. She moved
to London, where she eventually co-formed Anglo-American duo
The Dear Janes; the band released three albums and toured Europe
and the US. Her poems have appeared in magazines and anthologies
and she is the author of the first book-length monograph of
American poet Ruth Stone.
To the Boneyard is her first full collection.

Table of Contents

Greyhound

Wyoming rumbles under
swollen ankles. The lavatory door
clicks, the smell of piss hangs
by my face for a moment.
Cooling my cheek against
the window – I didn't expect snow –
I'm wishing for sleep
or a truckstop.
I am barren as the road.

The driver gives us twenty-five
minutes for coffee. Plates balance
like justice in the waitress's hands.
Under strip lights and gazes, elbows
propped on Formica, I inhale
caffeine steam, watch the sun
rise, the landscape thicken with white.

Home is ninety-three hours away.
I wonder what this place looks like
in the spring, how blue-cragged
those mountains will be.

As the sun begins pricking
prisms out of split-rail drifts,
I watch the bus grow
small, its exhaust
a blot on the snow.

Hustera

Open your legs — here
  is the gateway to hysteria,
a wandering of the womb,
  le ventre de la mère, surely
more like a breezeway
  to another room, a blow-through
on the way to the sea, the lunar
  push and pull, its waxing light,
crescent moods of our watery brains.
  Squat here, my little kumquat,
home of the giddy vibrations,
  birthplace of everything.

The search

I questioned everything alive –
beetles, daddy longleg spiders,
the crayfish at the bottom of the yard
in Mr Sampson's pond, the pond
that appeared and disappeared
with the rain and provided frogspawn
for my bucket. I kept it in the garage,
watching as it became small-tailed beings,
before the squatter bodies, their struggles
to evolve and survive without being
eaten by their own kind. The harm
lay in forgetfulness, and I don't remember
that they died; I can't recall what I did
with them. Perhaps I put them back
in the pond, or took them to school,
poor little black dots of anxiety,
their only world red plastic, seconds wide.

Cellular life

Mottled, I sit in my breathing
and rusty lungs, overcome with the measure
of today – my niece in a car crash,
her fractured spine; a cousin off his meds
in a foreign hospital; the daughter
of my brother's best friend
found dead with her boyfriend.
A thing in space, I cavort around myself like pond life,
clear body in which my blood is visible, my heart
on show. Giving away nothing,
the speed of travel across the water, the protection
of the glowing heart. It's not thinking,
it's the mind shut off, the body
moving for the movement of the body.
If I could see myself, I might seem desperate,
or at least frivolous, out on the surface
in my transparency, one of many
small red dots beating near each other
only to bounce away, skim, repelled, to another place
of rest, the space around me pulling and flowing,
prodded by rain larger than myself, craters
in water filling up with itself, I root
along the side of things, like salt in cracks
of skin, needles of time stoving in the fishing boats,
a swimmer gasping for air.

Considering why everything is out of place

In much the same way the field
holds on to its earth after harvest,
you and I hold the outside of truth –
the jutting sticks of summer, each
containing its share of ground,
sentries against erosion.
The endosperm gone, a few straw bales
remain. No core of argument, only
the shell of words before the door
slammed shut, echoes blasting
between the barn's thick walls.

The systematic upheaval of the interior

I was a tiny thing, a mixture of egg and shell
and beak, my limbs wrapped up. In a mirror
I always saw the person behind the person I was,
the one I didn't want. The edge of the mirror, the frame,
I could slip in there and confound my nerve.

The flagstones have loose lips: I always find them,
like homing beacons, the bones of my toes compete
for my vigilance, I curse my feet. People look,
I imagine, but without seeing a lack of grace.
From a distance, they might conceive I'm quite beautiful:

I've brought out my mirror-corner self and am suddenly
svelte, all tawny-haired-swinging and knees
to die for, ankles that narrow to accommodate
Balenciagas and a tattoo on the top of my right foot,
painful so close to the bone, the surface, worth every penny.

I sweep the face of the room, cling to some goddess's words
as she clambers before me onto the stage, ascends
the buffet table like a trapeze and we swing, drop,
catch each other's glances by the arms and land eventually
in the sawdust, stardust, whatever kicks up

from the sprung-wood floor. We're under a shadow big as the table,
perhaps under the table's shadow, the clink of crystal
and stilettos all around us, no one realising we've gone.
Someone's eyes stare into mine and I'm reliving a cliché
from my childhood, the one where I get rescued and kissed

until I relent, these half-baked secrets consistent with reality
as seen from the back of the mirror. What I remember most
is the hint of glass, of wood, the scent of cedar, my head
in that blanket chest, breathing it in, in, in,
exhaling round the room of my travels.

I want you

Uphill in lowest gear, the car decides
to stop with a crack loud as a cussword
in the middle of a conversation
with your Aunt May. I cross the stream on foot.

It's like walking through aspic, shreds of algae
ensnare my ankles like viridian guy ropes.
A strip of snakeskin's caught in the grass,
I fold it into a carnation for my buttonhole.

Dry land, there's a fork that shines
like an ambulance: I know by the sun
to take the left. Ahead is a racoon
weaving among the pines. I think *Rabies*,

throw bread from my sandwich in another
direction. I'm late, there's no signal
on my phone. I tell myself the car just needs oil,
that the *Gas-Rite* station's around that bend.

Opal

In 1995, my childhood drowned
under salt water and winds of a hurricane
named Opal. She didn't care, not for
a minute, that every book I'd ever saved,
from my father's copy of *Winnie-the-Pooh*
to Uta Hagen's *Respect for Acting*, had turned
into a mass of black and white pulp
that claimed baby teeth and Aunt Mabel's silver soap box,
my mother's cardigans, a charm bracelet
she'd given me when I was eleven – tiny
sterling cheerleader, ukulele, telephone, a pineapple
with a pearl in the middle; my grandmother's
embroidery that had hung above my baby bed:
Reap rich harvests that love has sown.

I learned to swim young, was betrayed by the ocean
only once before my mother dived in to rescue me.
After that, I never feared salt water,
even when my dad pointed out the barracuda
hovering nearby with its sideways eye,
signalled me through mask and snorkel to the shore.
My brother kept all the Hawaiian shells we'd collected –
the cowries, cones and volutes, the coral.
He gave me a basket of shells once,
now washed out with the books, the black
lacquered jewellery box my father brought
back from Japan, its ballerina
who danced on a mirror.

2.

Small sailboats glide across the sound,
unruffled as glass until a bow cuts
through. A blue crab scuttles along
the reedy bottom, the sand rich with clay.
I check the crab-nets, lower them back
in the water. Already there's a salty shimmer
of heat. A pelican, beak tucked, sits
on a pier-post, lets the breeze cool
its feathers. Underfoot, wood starts
to steam, softens the tar on my heel.

A bleached dinghy knocks against the piling,
slaps the sound, riding a far-off wake. I look
into the water, imagine I can see
my grandmother's hatpins among the reeds,
the minuscule ivory elephants
I would line up and count, never considering
they might not be passed on to my own
grandchildren. Never considering I might
not have grandchildren.

Beside the tiny herd, I wonder if those bits of sand
could be your ashes, loyal to the sound
where they were spread twenty years ago,
mingling with Dad's now. When he died,
I felt your absence. The way one death
brings back another. When we sold the house,

it was as though he had been torn away with it.
The way a hurricane can uproot even memories,
throw them miles from their starting place,
cover them until someone finds them.
The way time doesn't heal, it buries.

Pacific

The blue-black water, to think of
falling into it, the time it would take
from this height, from this speed,
falling past the portholes, past the
bingo-room and old Mrs Tulloch on
C-deck, past the chefs and the waiters
and the porters and the brooms, the
skeets boxed for shooting, the poker
chips in their crates, in time with the
sea-bird alongside the hull, beyond
the engine room and its lovely men,
some with beards, some bald, the cats
and dogs in kennels by the infirmary,
shuffleboard and glasses (with little
umbrellas and tiny plastic mermaids
or monkeys hanging on the rims)
abandoned by deckchairs, enough
time to say good morning to the
man in beige trousers like your dad's
before he goes upstairs with his club
to hit golf balls off the stern, the
time would slow down to allow all
that while you notice how very dark,
how very black is the blue you are
approaching in slow-motion, and
how just now, you had looked around
you and seen the sea as you see it now,
in all directions, the blue-black, the
deepest blue you have ever seen, in a
vast circle, and nothing else.

Great-aunt Constance

I feel heavy with years that seem to have come to this picture
of a young woman in a winter coat, contemplating
an ashtray on a table. It was the 1930s. Little money,
fewer jobs. An era, a relative I never knew.

I walk back and forth in the rooms of ancestors, climb
their ladders, even as I stiffen to the shouts of children outside
who fuck with my concentration and my aching broodiness.
I have a coat that same Copenhagen blue.

New York City is a communal photograph album,
memories blending until I'm not sure
what I remember and what I've only heard about.
You don't miss what you've never known. Not true.

My knuckles are red with cold. In the mirror my eyes
look so tired. I crumple a tissue into the ashtray,
turn to the window. That new high-rise blots out the skyline,
but around the corners a little light cuts through.

The straw

She caught insults and compliments in the same bar shift. When she wept at night, her lover told her he couldn't afford to lose more sleep. Her regular customers talked to her as though they'd traded barstools for therapy couches. She stood still to allow things to fly past. Some slid down her throat – her mother's death, an aborted child, her lover's bitterness in public places. They laddered up, unacknowledged, until her feet spread and her neck grew thick as a trumpeter's hitting high C. On the top of her head, in a scar where her hair parted, a crack began, in *tap tap tap*s like tiny hiccups; the crack became a hole, became a vertical gulch; phrases spouted upwards, exploded in Roman-candle shrieks. The sky was alight. Comments flowed through her. Tenses made no difference. Everything swallowed let loose.

Serial

All those nights of different lovers, thinking they wanted me
because I was special, they fucked me because they wanted to stay.
All that empty fucking that meant nothing and I thought it meant
something real was about to happen, as if fucking itself wasn't real at all.
The night Dominic said I was aloof I decided I wanted him,
to prove to him I wasn't, when every time before,
he'd come into the bar where I worked and I'd thought he was an idiot.
I'd make his Bloody Mary with extra horseradish anyway
and put him down to harmless. Began to see that maybe he was
a nice enough guy. But I didn't get why he attracted so many girls.
Then the aloof thing, in someone else's bar, and by god I'd show him.
He's one of the *D*'s I remember. I know there was a string of Daves
and a Dan, a Del and a Dean – whom I actually loved – and the other
letters seemed equally represented but the only time I put them
in an order was when I couldn't sleep. The *B*'s were weighty, the *M*'s
always a surprise – five Mikes, a Melody, a Mark or two – by the time
I got to the *N*'s, I was asleep. I couldn't count them because the number
kept changing, or I'd forget one, or one would get misplaced
and I'd have to slot him in. Later I found myself forgetting most of them
and faces would pop into mind with no identity,
floating by as I wondered who they were, if they were aggregates
of other parts of other faces, if any of them knew.
And the dark winters, the endings of nights I'd walk home,
the Upper West Side at three in the morning. I'd push through
new two-foot drifts and feel the cold begin to seep into the seams
of my boots, and the snow looked permanent under streetlights.

The edge of town

When we lived in the Great Cardhouse, we'd say,
and *which elephant is stomping with its buttery grey feet?*
Tarzan jokes would follow and we'd stand outside

the perimeter, eyeing the quarters on the pool table,
none of us daring to put our own coin on the corner.
Sometimes, on early afternoons when the bar was clear

of Springsteens (I imagined *Thunder Road* air guitar
rehearsals), we practised our own system
to see who could break the hardest

without skipping the cue ball off the table
like an errant satellite. Whoever could sink one
on the break was deemed *The Rancher* and gained

an extra beer. Balls missing the pockets by an inch.
We were consistent. Everyone scratched eventually
and was level on drinks when early evening came to.

We'd drop our session as the first of the slick-haired,
stubble-jawed hearthrobs sauntered in, checking out our asses
as we put the pool cues on the rack. We'd pick up our notebooks

and bottles of Pabst and find a table at the back,
wishing we could be cool all the time,
cool when other people were looking.

Fifth Floor Acute

Every night I draw up a schedule for the following day, in fifteen-minute blocks until 10pm meds. I lie, tell them I can't get tired. In nearby beds, women cry or moan or sometimes scream. Someone is snoring in minor thirds. Jackie has absconded again. I sleep only when it's almost dawn.

At 8am I mooch downstairs for powdered eggs. On sunny days I don't venture out. I roll cigarette after cigarette for my stock-box. I try not to speak. It seems my flesh is blown up like one of the dahlias in a Georgia O'Keeffe painting.

Jackie comes in after walking all night, cadges a cigarette. We blow smoke-rings, try to shape them in letters. I attempt the word *Dorothy* but it still looks like a stream of O's. She says *and your little dog too* and pokes her finger through one of the rings. I count my roll-ups and add two new ones.

Fluttering into the TV room, Thomas has metamorphosed into a World War Two streetwalker. When they bring out the watercolours, I ask a nurse if I can paint smoke. A worn chartreuse sofa sags under long fluorescent lights. All the visitors look as though they're suffering from something.

Billboards

Six years old in the back of a blue station wagon:
Holiday Inn. Esso. Walk a Mile for a Camel.
Burma-Shave. Home of Yellowstone.
Up front, maps full of words.

Curvy red and blue lines
led to cities – words first, then boulevards
and buildings. Later, I'd memorise white shapes
on green rectangles: *Sleepy Hollow Road*, *Runnell Avenue*,

Iroquois Point. Sing them like nursery rhymes
as my feet went round on the pedals. You taught me
to search for the perfect word,
that *Q* was useless without *U*.

I remember white-dotted avenues
on the table, the domino pile on the edge,
your voice singing *To the boneyard*
you must go, disembodied as any ghost.

Now you say *That's a good word*. Then
repeat it. As if you've never heard it. Now
we drive down roads I don't recognise.

The things we come down to

An ocean, a generation away,
his skyscraper-sized life scales down
to fewer and fewer windows and doors.

Over the phone,
he repeats phrases from a poster,
a keen boy decoding a map.

There are words
like manhole covers,
cracks of daylight and slam.

A figurine I gave him,
a manicure kit in a faux-lizard case,
his bifocals on a bedside table.

The viewing room

How can a man have flesh and be so cold?
They had filled your cheeks out, covered your body
with a blanket, its pattern of holes to trap warm air.
I resisted the impulse to see the Y-shaped scar,
run my fingers along it from sternum to abdomen.

I revisit this room over and over, wanting
paramedics to swarm in, pull down the blanket,
pound your torso, place gelled metal discs on your chest,
say 'Clear!' And the machine to make that almighty buzz
as your body jumps on the narrow bed. I'm here

for the flatline's fracture into waves, the breath-stopping blip
of a pulse. I unfold your ancient pea coat on my lap,
its wool stiff as Braille under my fingers.

Gift

The river L weaves through this town like a strand of blood
down your chin: thin, sneaking under bridges and beard,
curling past freckles of stones. You'd hardly know
it's there. Nearly dried up in parts, it's left a silty groove
where growth runs out of control. Sometimes it takes
a trick of light to recognise that any flow exists. Always
a surprise, that so much can spring from so tiny a nick.

Dad on a train

Il est dans ma tête toujours, toujours

The French countryside is not rolling,
it is flying by and my seat looks
backwards: with my slice of window

I only know where I've been.
All day I have seen him, as he was
laid out when I said goodbye, his face

with the merest bit of white between his lips
where they were glued as if he'd gone
to sleep after brushing his teeth

forgetting to rinse. I waited
for the blue blanket to rise and fall
knowing it wouldn't but nearly seeing it anyway,

as if it were suddenly last Thanksgiving
and I was checking on him
as he slept. For hours after, my lips tasted

chemical, were vaguely numb
where I had pressed them on his forehead, kissed
him three times because I couldn't believe

how cold he was.   Now I think of your books,
the ones perhaps I should have kept, and the yellow
cashmere sweater and I wish I could stop.

I've bought a beer from the restaurant car and
all I can smell is cigarette smoke in my hair.
How you'd grumble if we sat near a smoker.

On Sunday I wear his shirt

It's the only day he gets a look in,
is given a proper chair. Dad's shirt
is strictly for wearing indoors. It offers
comfort on a day which ought to be
a day of rest, not a time of guilt
for everything left undone.

One day, when I'm living
in the French countryside, bringing in
wood for the stove, or feeding the horse
I think I'll have, I'll wear it more
publicly. I haven't settled
into that age yet, when Dad's shirt

will grace my Levis, when I'll
cut my hair short, sport a fedora
and brown leather gloves.
I'll take my book down to the Vienne,
lie on that big rock in the river,
see his hands turning the pages.

Edit

In this version, you are still alive, and visiting us
in France. You are complaining about the heat. *This
is the life*, you say, but suggest air conditioning.

You sit, curved into an airport thriller, in front of the electric fan.
The light is dim between our two-foot stone walls, and in
profile you still look like Jeff Goldblum. You get up

and remix your martini, despite my efforts to hide
the ingredients you purchased in Duty Free.
What you would really like is a game of golf.

We take you to the river instead. I watch you swim,
your brown arms arching over the water like a stretch
of wings, see a younger you in the Gulf of Mexico,

hoisting up onto the pier, where the local pelicans,
your favourite bird, bristle the salt out of their feathers.
You climb the bank, knock the river out of each ear,

shake the water off your long arms. Refreshed,
you complain about the bruise from the river rocks,
the missed game of golf forgotten for now.

Sans sous-titres

Here could be almost anywhere, grass beaten to straw; pines and rows of poplars like dominoes blaspheme for the little rain stored at their feet. Unlikely *voisins*. Tiny saplings hunker down, pull the first plug. It's all going on underground. Madame Timonier's nectarines salivate on the dashboard, caravans comatose on the side of the road. Pylons walk alongside to Le Mans, from stillness to city. White cows blur past, desirable as hard-boiled eggs. *Je t'aime beaucoups* growls the Citroën but you try not to exceed 90, wonder if this Besançon – thirty-four kilometres ahead – is the Stendhal one. *White page! White page!* screams the grey stick of a tree as you hurtle by, dragging the muse by a bungee cord. *Milk!* responds the coffee as you enter *Centre Ville* and the pencil spills into that near-inaccessible place between the car door and the seat runner.

Murder

You get smaller and smaller
until you are nothing but a drop
of blood.

Across from the station is an element
clutching its atomic number, waiting for a name
before it fits on the chart.

It is anxious.

The circus next door has opened
its big top and the ringmaster's whip
is nowhere to be found.

There's a sardine looking
at the dust and a silver horse
without a saddle.

Hell is downstairs, door number 16.

It's only open during particular hours.
There are no appointments. You have
to show up and get lucky. It helps

if you can swim. Remember: you can't
get there from this spot. It's a surprise
where you end up. Sixty years on

you'll be singing in B-flat,
hitting the low notes you couldn't reach
when you were young.

It's easier than you think,
but you have to go gradually.

August in Préau

It's the sky that reminds me of Icarus. The clouds,
the way they move, and the handles of the idle plough
take on the shapes of legs, its coulter the body.
If only he'd float instead, drift into this field
where a farmer left his tractor, a patch of rust and red
against the dry grass, each blade thick and sharp, waist-high
in the spring. The plough's a sentinel with no food
until summer, its wheel a mill heating the cut hay.

Fires in the South of France have slowed with the storms,
but in our garden near the Vienne, words dry
before they reach the page. I consider the word *dearth*,
find *air* and *earth*, *water* and *death*, and the wind
that held Icarus as he flew, just for a moment,
into the senseless clouds.

Looking for Taylor and God in Chauvigny

i.m. T.H.

I stand between the yellow and the light
as if I am a pane of glass between
one form and another, the stained and leaded,
and the one created by explosions I cannot see,
fracturing on the surface of the sun.

High into a column is an eavesdropper,
a tiny stone face built to spy
on the congregation and the stragglers
who stumble upon this icy haven. I search
for more, but there is only one, the smallest
face of God, dropping out of the eaves.

My hand pauses over the font. I wonder if
it's a sin to touch Holy Water, to cross myself,
if a non-believer would crash into hell any harder.
Taylor would know these things. I turn my back
to God, and listen as the stone echoes
every breath, but the breaths are all mine.

If God *is* here, hovering over thoughts
of visitors to his cold house, perhaps his
is the voice of colour that detonates on the floor
through the stain and lead. And on days
when the light is silent, the little eavesdropper
closes his eyes while the gargoyles and the dragon,
on neighbouring columns, feast on cobwebs.

Route de la Tour au Cognum

i.m. H.R.B.

Scatterings of poppies by the *Route Nationale*,
the drought and rains finally subside
into late May sky. The family gathers
at the table, your only son at its head.
We re-tell stories, celebrate you
while each of us exposes a few strands
of what we were not, until now.
You are here and not here, the drought
now within the house you built, your chair
full of your lack – these things we struggle with,
and the desire to wake you from this unwavering
sleep, where you look as though at any moment
you might open your eyes and whistle,
as always, from the corner of your mouth.

Geometry

Cranes pull up shiny triangles
and fling them into the sun,
then pause against the sky,
as if to survey a city built with their shapes.

A sailor scans acres of water,
single drops splash
and dry on his arms
in peaked crystals of salt.

Beyond the docks, steel hulls roil
through shipping lanes, reflections
of constellations. Underwater trenches,
inverted pyramids of unknowable depth

point towards the centre of the earth.
We look at models of atoms, consider
images of hell, a devil
with an arrowhead at the end of his tail.

Beck and call

He arrived in a white Buick, torn leather seats
in the back. Three thousand miles without a map,
he'd headed north towards Quebec. Stopped
outside Bucky's café, downtown Main Street
in Springbok, Indiana, got the car wedged
between a '70s Schwinn tandem bike
and an El Camino, a book about coffins on the bed.

Her nametag said Rebecca. She held a box
of brown meringues, fresh from the baker next door,
set them on the counter, stuck a Bic ball-point
in her hair, took chalk from behind a bouquet, printed
Today's Outback Specials on the café blackboard.
He looked taken aback, asked 'Am I in Australia?'
and she giggled, her mouth like a little beak. His knees
vibrated like the humbucker pickup on his old guitar
and he hoped the tobacco stains didn't show on his teeth.

He felt like a prince in the house of the Bacchae, noticed
how shrivelled buckeyes flurried around telephone poles,
the tobacco-coloured floorboards bled bone
into the concrete buck where the mat rested outside,
Welcome to Bucky's. He wondered if Australia was so far
after all, a beaker of oil and a fryer on the stove,
Rebecca, the meringues, a baby crawling on the floor,

if he'd be *welcome* even with a bouquet when he drove
the red dirt home, Bic razor in his pocket, the smell
of a bake-off in the village, the house full of drawings
and noise. There'd be Rebecca in her best dress, small things:
a new book he didn't understand, a stormy spell
and a TV programme on Quebec. He would wonder
why he'd stopped in Springbok, Indiana, or if
all those bridges were still burning back in Daytona,
where he'd stolen his uncle's Buick on a bet, scared stiff.

Patty & Doug, 1970

She's sitting on his lap. He can't stop smiling,
as if the hand he holds contains a world
where the plumeria blossom in her hair
never wilts, as if they'll be sixteen forever.

She untucks her hair from behind her ear. It falls
against her cheek. She tucks it back again,
laughs at what he's said. She turns her face
to his. Their lips are new, and stutter as they
kiss. He tips his head back, sees the shells

in fishing-nets he suspended from the beams
of the lanai, can think of nothing romantic,
only *conch* or *cowrie*, *sea-fan*, *reef-coral*,
gecko. She laughs. He can't stop smiling.

Biloxi

Biloxi, where my mother was born,
where the Gulf of Mexico swerved for home,
Biloxi, whose lighthouse is framed on my wall,
whose largest live oak carried its legend
through generations of hurricanes:
the branch that was split by lightning,
the lovers who were parted by death,
reunited as the bough healed.
It left a hole in the middle to tell us
where we came from, where we're going.

Honolulu

If the wind picks up, it scratches
leaves like dry kisses against windowpanes,
chorus to the twenty-year scuttle
of cockroaches hatched and fed
on newspaper clippings in her desk.

White Venetian blinds await the fall
of grey Hush Puppies to shift this
room past mid-afternoon
where it is summer, always
summer, always two o'clock.

The daybed remembers her.
Plumeria blossoms through
the window, pristine white
and yellow strands of fragrance
to string in circles round her neck.

In hibiscus light, dust motes hang
before settling on pine. Fingers of a breeze
creep through from the kitchen, looking for skin,
for skirts to chase around her legs
until she laughs.

I-10

You drove the whole day without a whisper
of complaint while I dozed off and on
to the road's lullaby. Outside Madison
the radio became a bleat, and I tried
to find something we could sing to
until there was nothing.

As I lit both our cigarettes
I leaned into you, caught a hint
of the scent I'd known my whole life. It cut
through our smoke in those hours of highway
where we became ordinary, a mother and daughter,
neither one reaching towards a death

that would come too soon. We moved only
towards home, your wooden owls, the blueberry
pie on the kitchen counter, the known
things – your skin fresh with Revlon powder,
our sofa, the carpets – not the cold floors,
the white, long corridors.

Things my mother left unsaid

Once, when you were trying to finish
your embroidery, a gift to me, in your hospital bed,
I asked was there anything you wanted
to talk about; not just then, you said,
you were too tired. You never told me what you thought
about dying. I didn't press you. I knew
you believed God knew what He was doing,
that darkness was not what you would face
but the open arms of your grandmother and Aunt
Marguerite – whose eyes I have, you said,
who died when you were a child – this was your
unshakeable fact. If I pray, it is for your belief,
that you were spared the nothing I face: the daily
scramble on a dry hill, the earth-bound slide.

Longhand

I hold childhood report cards to my face
as if I could breathe her in with her signature.
The tiny notebooks full of jazz lyrics,
birthday cards, those loops and lines I memorised –
I hoard anything in her hand.

She scribbled in the margins of her old cookbook,
stuffed handwritten recipes between its pages,
one (for cornbread) in my own eleven-year-old script.
On the inside cover is her recipe for perfect piecrust
which I have never tried to follow.

I was married at her bedside: her yellowed eyes
moving in and out of focus, my fingers worrying the lace
on my palms, wedding vows in counterpoint
to hospital intercoms. She witnessed the marriage,
her final signature unreadable.

Sunlight in a nearly empty room

i.m. M.D.

Except for that spot where the sun shines
through the window, the floor is cold.
You could stand there until the world moves
that bit farther and the light grows

too thin to warm. You're all bones now —
your body has abandoned you in this.
There's no bed anymore, only the steel chest
of drawers, taking up a whole wall.

A pencil rolls across the floor.
You follow it, you and your bones,
your empty flesh, your cold hands.
You put your ear to the door.

It's like standing beside a seashell —
there's the sea, whishing, whispering,
Come in, come in, come in. But you're
already in. The sea is outside, surely.

Octavia

From the time we could see, there were the tomatoes.
Rich in their skins, on her kitchen table.

Even when it rained. They turn our eyes inwards. There
is a dark that stands in corners.

At the thick wooden counter, allowed the big knife at last,
we sliced according to her instructions. Soon

we were not sure: was that the school recess bell? When
we'd be chosen for teams? Are we desirable?

The girl, whose smile drew me – had I
existed before I was her friend? Sometimes

there is a mistake. We call it our imagination. Start
slowly, in mustard-yellow circles until

you reach the hollow centre. It is a dark place.
There is no one else.

Let the tomato slip carelessly from your hand.
Be ready. Let it fall.

Stepdaughter

From your kitchen I watch her, blonde and two,
digging with you in the napping flowerbed
where every shifting bit of earth makes room

for sleeping winter breaths curled like thumbs in fists,
thumbs in mouths. She laughs, flings a toy-spade
of dirt, jumps on worm-mounds, practises squeals.

We stack wood on the fireplace and see it burn
before we feel it. How strange that blue is deepest
heat as well as deepest water, that flame stays
on the periphery of wood as a whitecap on the sea.

and all that blood and then nothing

as if all that remained had been
carried away in one drawn out tide

you count the dry days until you forget
the exact date and words and names

these things too are slipping
you find yourself waiting only this time

what's desired may be impossible
so you begin to think of it as bereavement

recalling all those winters
when there was only you with time

enough for summers and seawalls
and the slap of small bare feet

Lack

Underneath the repetitions
fish take the river with them, run
northwards past the power station,
make their own electricity;
the whirr of the helicopters disintegrates
in near-silence, tendons shift
under strain, the longing for release
like the desire for a baby
and words are unhinged, their only
sentence as long as a freight train
stalled, a vast iron lump on the tracks.

My stepdaughter's room

I stand just inside the door, as though
going further will mean I might not
make it out again. In front of me, the blue rug,
its edges lined in stodgy dust. Her doll sags
on the cushion in an uncompleted somersault.
I must walk past, understand
that this is not for me, this broken gaze,
this shuttered dalliance. Where her bed waits,
overdue library books are askew. Beside it,
the Etch A Sketch swims in its own grey sand,
the outline of an impossible round face, the mouth
a straight line. The crush of air just a little
too tight. Her only pair of dungarees,
outgrown, balled up on the chair, two
small bears, marble eyes towards the wall.
I hear the creak of floorboards beneath my feet,
her voice from the kitchen below. Her bag sits
on the bedside table: fake hair extensions,
mascara, opaque foundation. Downstairs,
her mobile phone active to her touch,
password, username; locked.

Kefalonia

On the flight home together, he was quiet,
already absent, editing her out of the tales
he would relate to his wife.

That reckless summer, he could make no other choice
and she was blind beyond the holiday,
her life contained in its two weeks.

They'd found a beach, inaccessible by land,
made love against their rented boat, she
doubled over the bow. They dared anyone to discover them.

At night, shooting stars competed with the thickness of cicadas
and wet slaps against the docks
where fishermen beat the octopuses.

They drank Ouzo out of plastic cups, ate tomatoes and sardines.
She swam every Ionian cove they could find,
back and forth its entire width,

and again the next day, to make it more real.
Each bay disappeared
as soon as they mounted the hill to the road.

During supper at the taverna, she fed kalamari
to the feral cats under the table. She could feel
the prickle of fleas on her skin.

They shot whiskey in Harry's Bar, clambered up terraces
of olive groves, sailed into Fiscardo.
On their first holiday, the world was ancient.

Post-op

The cuts did not heal as quickly as we'd understood
and the stitches kept popping, things kept falling out
of the gash: some days it would be a heart,
first mine, then yours in sympathy, then other organs,

slipping to the floor like recalcitrant children
in a supermarket. They began to be an embarrassment,
to show up at all the wrong times:
a lung in the library, a spleen on a crowded bus.

The close calls. Once, I saw your wife
in a post office queue, and it was all I could do
to stop the bleeding – I held my wrists
against each other and ran out.

Over time, things settled down. My hand stopped
sliding to the phone, my tongue stopped burbling
but I love you and my lips got tough, ceased
to let words through. I stay at home now.

I still have the odd moment when my liver insists
it's the end, and my eyes join in for a while.
And sometimes there's this phantom pain
from my left ribcage down to my hip.

That summer window

Every time you look through there are new
shoots, small pale leaves. At the drop

of the blossom is a fruit beginning, tiny head capped
with bristle, holding on to the branch

with a sliver of neck. As green deepens, late
in June thickness, the inches between become less

sure of the light, until it is suddenly non-light,
edging towards the clutch of moonlessness. The glass

is gone now. Leaves stretch to the bed. The branch
bends to find you, as you think you're asleep,

as it knows you are not, and you look from grey to grey
to the puny silences of light catching through

the bottom of the door, you wrench off the covers and cannot
see the way out, while the little neck

creates a whirr of sound as it whips past your ear, and you
swing one last time on the flickers of the wall

before you ease yourself onto the branch, where you will
wait until September to fall.

Interior

It is a Wednesday night.
Evinrude, next door's cat,
runs into our house
soon as the door opens,
just a crack and she's in,
a brown streak with her outboard purr.
There's a light on
in the corner and the shutters
are open, the night air
pulls at the flame on the stove,
makes it stutter. You walk by me
and say nothing. I say nothing back,
pour some wine into the soup.

My mail on the table
is a white stack that's grown
by the day. When I lift it, a clutch
of envelopes slips to the floor,
catches your attention.
As you kneel beside me
there's a second when this
is enough: our hands
as we gather up letters,
the cat as she rubs against my elbow,
the sound of our breathing
when nothing is unsaid.

Lover

I cannot melt into you, I cannot become you,
though the flat of my hand knows
how the hairs on your thigh stand up, like grass
when it goes spiky in July, half-scratching the tender
middle of my palm, and my fingertips know

the skin between your shoulder blades,
smooth as kid-leather gloves, but it is not my skin
although sometimes the weight of your hands
holding my wrists on the pillow just before
your fingers lace through mine like weeds

is so familiar, the lines on your palms as they run
over my forearms press maps into me,
and your face is as only *I* will ever see it, and so close
I almost forget that you are not me,
that what I see is more than a reflection.

On departure

The rainwater on the ground beneath my window
flashes like growth on a time-lapsed film – not ripples,
but swathes of shallow water across the runway.
The airplane is being buffeted before we even take off.
I want to turn to you, say *Whatever happens, I love you*,

so we have that at least, if not our hand luggage,
house keys, passports, my new laptop, as we plunge
into the icy ink of the English Channel, La Manche,
The Sleeve we say, and think of ghost stories. And you and I,
not on either side but sinking in the middle,

must make a new name for it, our burial, our part of the water
that is neither here nor there. Before our bodies are found,
across a bigger sea, my relatives will be unaware
they should mourn us, that we have been dead
while they have been going about their days.

For them we will have died on another date, the time difference
changing the night into morning, and in their nescience
we will remain alive a bit longer, perhaps
spending those extra days somewhere within the oxygen
of the ocean, breathing underwater as we once did.

Nearing Dieppe

That cow looks lame, stands hunched up like a cat,
stick-legs balancing its car-sized body.
Forty-five kilometres to go and the adaptor dies,
so our ten-year-old abandons her portable DVD
and settles for a book on how to be the best at everything.

This is our last trip in the 2CV and we're sensitive
to every judder, every fume, every click that comes
out of the engine. It's the narrowest of cars,
requires us to sit shoulder-to-shoulder, thigh-to-thigh.
From now on it will be more of a stretch

to reach my hand to your leg. The ride will be quieter –
not only road noise is muffled –
and we'll sail by those cows too fast to notice
how frail their legs look, how we've stopped touching.

Lerot

There is nothing. No one else here. And then the lerot inside the roof scrambles above my head in the smallest hours of the morning. If he were to seek water, the roof would be clear of scratching creatures in the middle of nowhere in the middle of the night. There is tranquillity only in the daytime here, where the kestrel hunts and the lerot sleeps. But at night the bats come out of the eaves, the owls swoop over our windscreens in a huge white wash of body and feathered majesty and the rodent that lives under our roof wakens and shifts inches from our sleep and pulls us into the nocturnal world, the creatures of prey. I must poison him.

(A lerot is a type of dormouse prevalent in southern Europe and northern Africa)

Poem with certain lines stolen from Raymond Chandler
or Taking life seriously with Philip Marlowe

I sit at the client side of your desk while you
study yesterday's dust on the venetian blinds
and the expiring bee on the windowsill who's flown
too many missions. Your pipe threatens to go out
if you don't pay attention to it and I wait for you.
It isn't your mouth, particularly, though I like it
very well. It isn't the table of your shoulders –
and I've nestled a few hours in the right crook already –
or how quickly you can introduce a man to the taste of floor.

The telephone rings; someone offers you a small piece of money
to watch his neighbour – catch her poisoning his dog.
I can hear him curse when you refuse. It's more a job
for the Tailwaggers, you say, and he says, 'Nuts to you, big shot,'
and slams down the phone. Then a girl oozes in – hair
like a silver fruit bowl – and wants you to throw a scare
into her roommate. She can't pay you; she figures you
can do this one gratis. You won't. 'You're no gentleman,'
she shrills. And maybe it's in your reply

when you tell her, 'Where does it say I have to be?'
that sets my insides going like the window cleaner I saw walk up
the skyscraper wall that day – but all I know is I came in here
feeling like a short length of chewed string and now
I look at you, as you run your hand along your chin
and for the three hundredth time, swear you'll never again
use an electric razor. You watch me light an extra cigarette,
reach across to brush away the dead bee now spread-eagled
on the corner of the desk. The traffic brawls endlessly.

Beginning ballet over forty

I think *yes, I have it*. The pas de valse is slow
but winning. And then she wants a pirouette
in the mix and, in the room, I'm the tornado,
dizzy and feeling like I've been caught

stumbling in my underwear, a dipsomaniac
on the sprung-wood floor. I know she won't
believe me when I say it was fine at home –

there, I have about as much room to practise
as a mouse in a milk jug; quality
must count for something. It's like following
the cracks in the pavement and not

stepping on them for fear of breaking
your mother's back. Only the cracks are never
a pace wide anymore, and it's my back now.

From a rocking chair in Brooklyn

In Paris in 1927, we kept the Kreagers' penguin for three days,
her little black and whiteness waddling like a skittle down the hall.
We were teaching her to sing, but they came to get her back. Found us
on M. Decoute's funeral train – in the refrigerated *voiture*? –
giving Hester a bath. The coffin was fishy where she'd walked.

Hefty fine, but we had a calling. Then the unhappy leopard cub
from the *Jardin*; we coaxed it right to us through that hole in the fence.
Sweet little boy cub, all tumble and spot. We were on our way
to Perpignan – figured he needed a warmer climate for the winter –
when he ran at the waiter and pinched all the duck off the tray.

The waiter wasn't telling him not to, though. Anyway, we had to
give him up. When we got out, I took a fancy to tarantulas:
they're small enough to keep in a beauty case with room for comfort.
This exotic animal and bird show came through Toulouse,
and there was Maria, a Chilean bird-eating rose tarantula,

or some such. Like a tiny-waisted eight-legged kitten
without the ears, I thought. Delicate girl. They put her
on my wrist and she walked up my arm and it felt like rain.
Fitz distracted her keeper. Oh she was lovely. Liked mice too,
which was convenient. After a few weeks

we thought we'd get her a companion, and heard about
Arthropods of Andorra and headed south. But the Pyrenees were brutal,
so much snow, and Maria became all listless and floppy.
More like hail than rain. Went off her mice.
So we steered towards Spain, thinking that at least

they'd speak her language, but they inspected her case
at the border and took her away. Made us leave France.
See those boards across the way, and the chimney? That's what's left,
but all winter we had the fire going. Calvados! Marshmallows!
Look, I've nearly finished this arm. Fitz's favourite blue.

Cat, Dog and Desire

Today, I watch the oldest ginger cat in the neighbourhood, tufty matted fur, large belly drooping as though empty of the last brood. She finds the warmest spot left on the concrete courtyard, slowly lowers herself and gives over to it, rolling once on her back, paws batting the air. Almost as soon as she's there, she's back again on her feet, wobbling off out of (window) frame. Desire is not dependent on one thing or the other. That time I saw the wire-haired fox terrier and smiled at its owner as I passed. The dog looked like Asta from the Thin Man films, and I imagined myself as Myrna Loy with William Powell. Desire. I desire a dog and a cat. But how do you write about desire of a dog – it seems somehow feeble, less than the wantonness of human desire, which is eminently writable. People assume everyone seeks *someone*, there's a space set aside for it, it's part of one's status: *Looking for* _____. No one ever writes *dog*. Or *cat*.

Kitchen Blues

She says I lead a vanilla sort of life, fed up
like the hens with the comfort of Friday.
I don't know what you mean, I tell her,

and it's true. I scrape by again and again, nearly asleep
in my habits, my nerves. Nights are harder, everything
stills down and you can hear the earth tick.

She's like a child with her head in a full fridge,
popping up with the odd word, unmoved
as the devilled eggs fall, dismantle on the floor.

Dry

Until now, I can't remember a time it didn't rain.
The roof is disharmonious when I write.
Singing doesn't work. It can't compare –
the cadence is boneless, no contrapuntal drips, time
ticks unevenly. The air is vertiginous. My ears cannot wring
enough sound out of the space around me and there's no water to

bring the dust down. I have *another* papercut; two
cats are fighting out back, the pollen is rising and quackweed reigns
over everything. But I've mastered the strimmer – I can ring
the azaleas, edge the path. I've cut the thorns right
down (now I suffer blackberry guilt). The garden's heady with thyme
though some evenings are still chilly: dew-frost lit on the pear

last week; it should be blossoming – there's a pair
of buds waiting to open. I might buy a beagle to
keep me company. The Mitts' dog had six this time.
On the horizon tonight, there's heat lightning, a storm with no rain
like last summer. Night fishing. Doesn't seem right
without you: craters like pumice, the moon's hazy ring

like a streetlight through chlorine-washed eyes, a ring
of smudgy rose-blue glow – I can't pare
this down, how can I write
about this so it's clear? I walk barefoot, too,
sponge-toe my feet in the dry grass, do rain
dances every morning at breakfast-time.

The neighbours think I'm nuts. Remember the time
we lay on our backs with binoculars, swore we could see rings
around Saturn? Fell asleep on the grass until it started to rain –
we saw thirteen snails by the door, and one mating pair,
all positioned like a crawling army obstacle course, heading to-
wards the cool damp of the brick wall, performing some seasonal rite…

Everything sprang from us, I thought, that was what *right*
meant. I had it right this time.
I never doubted it, I still never do, I'm never in two
minds. I believe those bells at St Anselm's when they ring
but I feel a bit sad when I see even pigeons in pairs,
try to imitate their coo-sounds. I wish it would rain.

I'll try to get this right: without rain,
time falls most heavily, I am pared
down to my thinnest skin. Please ring.

Restaurant hunting in Nashville

I should have known, when you tied me to a chair with gaffer tape, that you hadn't meant breakfast. It took me that long, between laughing — and snorting, when that didn't work, through the two-inch silver bonds of your choice, *sir* — to understand that it would be some time before French toast. A slip of the tongue at the bar, and the idea entered me as delicately as a snowflake; I didn't feel it until I was in my hotel. It persisted like a sewing machine and I tapped out your number on the phone, got a taxi and there I was, at your door, before you could say *lights out*. It was the prospect of breakfast that drew me, I thought, as you pulled off my clothes and began with the adhesive. There's only so much one can do, fastened to a chair, so we did that, or rather you did and I responded in a limited fashion. Eventually, of course, you cut the bindings and I was grateful for the bed, although not tired. You fell asleep, still no sign of breakfast. So I dressed and went in search of the all-night diner and its perfect egg.

Camouflage ponies on a train from Weymouth to Waterloo

My friend Carole has a handbag made of ponyskin,
dyed camouflage green and black. We discuss this,
how is it different from cow leather. *Smell it*,
she says. It smells horsey, that warm, sun-on-hay
smell. The leather is soft, melting under my fingertips.
It's impossible, though, not to see ponies in that field,
picture ponies at the fair or ponies at Gerry Cottle's circus,
children riding, children desperate, but as soon as they are
within petting distance, children terrified.
But camouflage ponies are different. They fit
right into a child's world. When you think
your children are playing make-believe, they are riding
camouflage ponies. The train bumps into Basingstoke,
something falls against my shoe. *Careful*,
says Carole, *Pony landing on your feet*.

Definite article

The pencil the paper the lines the forearm
the hand the fingers the knuckles the tendons
the bones the muscles the compulsion the lessons
the handwriting paper the graphite on off-white
the spaces the spaces between the letters
the words the lines between the pages
the synapses the oxygen the cut-off point
the freeze the fear the distraction the memory
the grief of others the lack of function
the lack of care the brain shutting down
the loss of the mind's eye the lapse of the tongue
the who the why the where the when
the loss of control of movement of cause
the loss of effect the dark the light
the flicker the shadow the eyelids the cheekbones
the fall of the chest the heartbeat the drift
the outbreath the stillness the stillness the

Din

i.m. C.W.

You grip my shoulders in the dark of the audience:
your upper arms, all biceps and sinews, those leaps
of taut flesh keep you apart up there in the lights,
your body curved over your guitar as it feeds back.

You think you've met me before.

I find you in Morton Street in your matt red living room,
your mother's sculptures around the fireplace.
It's your eyes I remember most, those round brown eyes
staring until your focus shifts.

I join you later at your corner bar, you're eating a pork chop
the cook set aside for you. We shoot tequila, hold hands
and walk to Washington Square so you can score some pot.
You say I can have anything I want and you play me
Visions of Johanna and Little Walter records until dawn.

It's 6 o'clock in the morning when you finally kiss me.
You don't fit anywhere else, your voice is the gravel
that sends me to sleep, slaps me awake and you don't answer
my letters, the postcards with the lizard & his bifurcated tail,
the seashells, my small writing

and the last time I see you
in the hotel you call me beautiful and the lights are up full
and your eyes, unblinking, are clear and brown and huge.

I listen to *Dirt Floor* and start again at the beginning,
put it on a loop so it's all I hear; your National Steel, its digs
and scuffs, leans against the wall by your door.

Fire

We have on this earth criers of the silence of our lives –
the hesitant clamour of bees to the hive, syrup that drains
from a wound into a bucket by your bed, the IV flood

into your forearm. On the other hand, consider how hard it is
to be a victim, how you must work at it even when you begin
to heal, children around your sofa complaining about schoolwork

they're unable to finish because you are ill. The link that flies
into your daughter who will remember the drip as well
as the classroom boards with their fuzzy words. What can be inferred

is the hum of computers, out-of-range radio stations, a mix
of conclusions from Joan of Arc to Wyatt Earp, as dust
tumbleweeds under the table. If you don't understand

your prayer doesn't always get answered, perhaps that's why
your fingers get burned. So why have you lit a match to the barn?
What good is the gun in your left hand? In *The Magnificent Seven*,

Eli Wallach had to look down to find his holster; that split-second
could mean death, but no one shoots the man
in the middle of the script if he has lines all the way to the end.

I Am Young

I am not young. This is a strange thing. I surprise the mirror, remind myself, *I am not young*. But I am not convinced. *I am young*, I say to myself. I argue without saying anything. And then I see someone my age wearing something I might have worn twenty years ago and I think *No. I would not wear that now.* And I know, then. I am almost persuaded. I walk quickly alongside a young woman and I forget again. I see a woman in the shop window: all that time, germinating. It's a puzzle. That boy there, leaning against the train door. *I would have fancied him*, I think, just after I think how nice he looks, how I very nearly fancy him now. I should tie a string around my finger. I forget so much.

As rain lashes the corrugated roof

In the underbelly, there is a lot to be getting on with.
Contemporary life slots in right alongside
the stick-and-carrot onrush of the decade, its evangelical

genetics. There is no sleep without earplugs, no dreams
without the past, a younger me with new temptations
and halls that lead into doorless bathrooms. I wake

to see if my neck is collapsing: this will be the point
of no return, where the only smooth skin beneath the jawline
is in a dream of a public shower, with other young

women attending to my every need. I am both commander
and plaything, submissive on the tiles, oblivious to the gales
slamming against the windows.

Manhattan interlude

I am in a lift, heading up to the forty-fifth floor, to Russell's apartment, 45-O, the studio apartment with the grand piano, the windows overlooking midtown Manhattan. On windy nights you could feel the building sway, ever so slightly. On cold nights – how many were there? – he lit a fire. I remember a fireplace, although it's possible there wasn't one. We'd make love, silently, because I was too shy to speak once my clothes were off. I thought my body should be able to say enough, to say all I couldn't, the words sliding off my body onto the bed, into the air, on our sweaty limbs as they coasted over each other – it's no good. I can't remember much about us back then. I do remember he made me scream once – that may have been the first time I'd ever had an orgasm with someone inside me – but that was in my shared apartment on the *eighth* floor, a West End Avenue sublet, books lining the walls of the curving entry hallway, where the two rooms radiated off. There was a piano there, too, but it was in bad need of a tuning, which my roommate and I could never afford, and the real tenants were living elsewhere, in Europe or someplace I only dreamed about at the time. Russell went on the QE2 from New York to London, where they had grand pianos ready for him. That January it snowed a lot and I waited for him to call me. I knew when he was returning but he didn't call for another week. The next winter he said he was getting married. Since I hadn't ever been able to talk to him in a way that didn't involve my body, I wasn't surprised, but I felt my heart craze against my stomach when he told me. I went to the pre-wedding party, a posh event in a huge uptown apartment. I don't remember anything about it except what I wore, and I expect I drank too much. My friends thought I was mad to go. I moved to London the following summer. Now I look him up on the internet and of course he has no idea.

Where we are

I saw for the first time how fallen leaves
get pressed into the road, perfect stencils. They'll be
rubbed off, bit by bit, the cars and trucks rolling
over them every day, until they become dots of yellow,
those delicate veins still running through.

Pensacola Beach Bridge

I would cross it each new summer, a toll bridge
with a hill in the middle to let boats through,
the dolphin sign a carnival pointing the way.

I'd throw coins in the basket, hear the rattle and *ding!*
before the striped arm went up.
The old bridge sat alongside, its draw removed.
Fishermen lined its rails, gulls dived for scraps.

Everything eased, like my brown legs into sand.
Hard bodies, new drugs, I crossed over to them
with the songs on the radio — *Take Me to the River*,
What a Fool Believes, *How Do I Survive*.

Last September, a storm with a boy's name
destroyed it. Photographs show great chunks gnashed away
en route to the remnants of Oriole Beach, Palafox Street.

The birds calling over Pensacola Sound don't know
how the seasons rush, single days like the fish
they swoop down upon.

Perhaps there's no bridge to anywhere we've been.
All those stars we see that no longer exist.
In the blaze of the September sun, the glints
on the still water under what remains.

Stealing from Borges: Me and her

The other one, the one called Barbara,
is the one things happen to. She sits back
on the settee while I get the dinner
on the go; I taste the rush in every bite
even though I starve myself. I am the one
to do all the washing in the house,
extra if there are guests, but she gets all the credit.
My niece hugs her rather than me, although
I hand-washed her favourite shirt
and ironed her new trousers
but Barbara has the knack of waltzing
through the room just in time
to collect the affection. I keep her glasses
clean and she never thanks me
and she sits on the back of the bike
so I have to pedal us both;
my body should be improving all the time
but she's the one to benefit.
And the things that come out
of her mouth! I feel my face getting hot
but she takes no notice. I don't know what
she's trying to prove. It's me the lines come from,
but there they are on the page,
in her workshop, plagiarised. The hand
holding the pencil – I can't tell if it's hers
or mine. She yawns from boredom,
I yawn from exhaustion.

Carmel Valley Road

for D.M.

Most people, when they've drowned, don't live.
You had pulleys and levers, and contraptions to enable you to
        hold a fork
and sign your name. When I touched down in Monterey,
there you were, with your hand-controlled van, its ramps
sliding out the back at a button's touch.

You took me down 17-Mile Drive,
past Alfred Hitchcock's garbled house, to where the seals bark
on the smooth rocks while the Pacific crashes
on the suicide crags, like the opening shots of *Peyton Place*
my mother would never let me watch.

On Carmel Valley Road, in your flat with its wide hallways
and low counters, I grilled swordfish for supper my second night
and you uncorked the wine with your teeth.
Afterwards, in the communal garden, you showed me
the stargazer lily you had planted in my honour.

The next day, they were changing the road signs
near the highway as the dust rose from the ground
on our walk to the riverbed. I stood
beside your chair, one hand on the back of your neck,
Carmel River jade glinting off the boulders.

We talked about chickens, your van, the dried-up spine
of river. I meant to say, *It's not just you.*
In my *dreams, you walk, too.* I wanted to feel the grip of your hands
on my waist, my caught breath, our careless, stupid power.
I wondered how many people knew how tall you are.

Our phone calls trickled out. Years later, rushing through town
on tour, I passed Carmel Valley Road.
Traffic was jammed down to the shore, and beyond
well-bred dogs and clicks of tourist cameras,
surfers sat on the glass of the Pacific.

Acknowledgements

Acknowledgements are due to the editors of the following publications, in which some of these poems appeared: *Magma*, *The North*, *Brand*, *The Interpreter's House*, *Paris Lit Up*, *nth Position*, *Limelight*, www.englishpen.org, *The Poem*, *Catechism: Poems for Pussy Riot* (English PEN, 2012), *I am Twenty People!* (Enitharmon, 2007), *This Little Stretch of Life* (Hearing Eye, 2006), *Images of Women* (Arrowhead, 2006), *Gobby Deegan's Riposte* (Donut, 2004), *Four Caves of the Heart* (Second Light, 2004), *Making Worlds* (Headland, 2003), *Parents: an anthology of poems by women writers* (Enitharmon, 2000).

'The search' won second prize in the SCJ Poetry Award 2013.

My gratitude to Sheenagh Pugh, Philip Gross and John Stammers for invaluable advice and support. Thanks also to members of the Group for their comments, particularly to Judy Brown for her immeasurable help and generosity. I am grateful to Don Paterson, Mark Doty, Mimi Khalvati, Stephen Knight, Michael Donaghy, Carrie Etter and Myra Schneider for valued guidance, and Sophie Mayer, Katy Evans-Bush, Fawzia Kane, Clare Pollard, Tamar Yoseloff and Liane Strauss for wisdom and input. Huge thanks to Sue Parkhill, Anders Kjaergaard, Tamara Tracz, Judy Bould, and Susan K. Muir. Special thanks to Ruth Stone and Marcia Stone Croll, and to Steve Betts, always the first editor.

And Todd Swift, Holly Hopkins and Edwin Smet – I can't thank you enough.

EYEWEAR PUBLISHING

EYEWEAR POETS

MORGAN HARLOW MIDWEST RITUAL BURNING
KATE NOAKES CAPE TOWN
RICHARD LAMBERT NIGHT JOURNEY
SIMON JARVIS EIGHTEEN POEMS
ELSPETH SMITH DANGEROUS CAKES
CALEB KLACES BOTTLED AIR
GEORGE ELLIOTT CLARKE ILLICIT SONNETS
HANS VAN DE WAARSENBURG THE PAST IS NEVER DEAD
DAVID SHOOK OUR OBSIDIAN TONGUES
BARBARA MARSH TO THE BONEYARD
MARIELA GRIFFOR THE PSYCHIATRIST
DON SHARE UNION
SHEILA HILLIER HOTEL MOONMILK